Preceding pages: *The Banarasi saree continues an ancient tradition of excellence in handwoven fabrics. Ancient Romans, records reveal, valued a high quality muslin produced in Varanasi. Today, the Bana saree, an essential part of an Indian bride's trousseau, is exported th world over. A close up of the* zari*—gold and silver thread woven int intricate patterns.*

Inset on page 2: *Ram Lila, the annual dramatic enactment in a folk style of the life story of Lord Ram marks the high point of the festive season in September-October. A character from the Ram Lila seen with his mask.*

The Shiva linga is worshipped as an emblem of a god beyond human comprehension. For the Hindu it represents the still point of the turning world. A view of an open air Shiva linga on the Harish-chandra Ghat.

Pramesh Ratnakar

Lustre Press

Delhi ◇ Banaras ◇ Agra ◇ Jaipur ◇ The Netherlands

The Spirit of the Place

With a recorded history of 3000 years and an unrecorded one that stretches into mythology, Varanasi, located on the western bank of the Ganga in Uttar Pradesh in north India, is one of the oldest living cities in the world. Named after two rivulets, Varna and Assi, that mark the northern and the southern boundaries of the city, Varanasi is also widely known by two other names—Banaras and Kashi.

Three dimensions of this ancient city stand out.

First, there is the extraordinary continuity of its religious and cultural traditions. When Mark Twain visited Varanasi at the end of the nineteenth century he quipped, 'Varanasi

Facing page: *Renouncers belonging to the Juna Akhara camping on the Harishchandra Ghat. The posture, with thumbs on forehead, is a mark of obeisance to the guru or deity. In the Hindu tradition, the renouncer seeks spiritual salvation outside the social framework, emphasizing non-action and non-desire, as opposed to the duties and the multiple appetites of the social man.*

A young initiate wearing an impressive rudraksha*—necklace made up of holy beads.*

The Dasashwamedha Ghat, located roughly midway on the river front, is easily the city's most accessible and the most popular ghat. Dasashwamedha, meaning 'Ten Horse Sacrifice', was considered to be the most auspicious of all ritual sacrifices in ancient times. The mythical king, Divodasa, is said to have performed the sacrifice here, with Lord Brahma himself as his priest.

Cremation rites are followed by 12 days of shraadh *rites to help the soul make its journey to the world of its ancestors. Hindus from all parts of the country come to the city to cremate their dead and to perform* shraadh. *A group of pilgrims*

from south India are seen honouring their ancestors with offerings of food and water during a shraadh *ceremony.*

is older than history, older than tradition, older even than legend, and looks twice as old as all of them put together.'

The fact, however, is that some of the most antiquated buildings in the city are no more than 200 years old. The city was more or less rebuilt after its repeated sacking by invaders in the medieval period. The 3000 year old past exists in Varanasi not in monuments but in the day to day practices of its people. The life, culture and the beliefs of the people of Varanasi hold up a mirror to the evolution of Indian civilization. If one can imagine Beijing, Athens or Jerusalem still resonant with the intellectual, cultural and ritual traditions of ancient times, it is possible to understand the tenacity with which Varanasi has kept alive its age old traditions.

Sherring, an Englishman, writing about Varanasi in the mid-nineteenth century pointed out:

Facing page: *Special merit is meant to accrue to those who perform the sacraments of the life cycle,* samskaras, *on the holy ghats of Varanasi. A mother, with her new born baby, is seen performing one of the sacraments. The black mark on the child's forehead is meant to ward off the evil eye and ill fortune.*

A woman praying at the Dasashwamedha Ghat.

'Twenty-five centuries ago, at the least, it was famous. When Babylon was struggling with Nineveh for supremacy, when Tyre was planting her colonies, when Athens was growing in strength, before Rome had become known or Greece had contended with Persia, or Cyrus had added lustre to the Persian monarchy, or Nebuchadnezzar had captured Jerusalem, and the inhabitants of Judaea had been carried into captivity, she had already risen to greatness, if not to glory.'

The second major point of curiosity is that though the city has undoubtedly played a decisive role in the evolution

The traditional Sanskrit name of Varanasi is Kashi or the Luminous One . They say Kashi is the place where the eternal light of Shiva intersects the earth. The light in the city is said to possess a special quality. It illumines reality and shows the way to the ultimate truth.

of Indian civilization, it was never, like Athens or Rome, a major political power.

Varanasi dominated the Indian cultural landscape on the basis of its

Facing page: *They say the people of Varanasi celebrate 13 festivals in a 7 day week. During the festival of Makar Sankranti in January, a bath in the Ganga is a must and the ghats remain busy with bathers all day long.*

The dawn is the city's best hour. Everyday thousands of worshippers and bathers gather on the river front and greet the rising sun with salutations like 'Har, Har Gange' and 'Har Har Mahadev' or the chanting of the famous Gayatri mantra. A devotee, knee deep in water, is seen paying homage to the rising sun.

religious and intellectual power alone. From ancient times the city has been the foremost centre of Hindu pilgrimage as well as a seat of Sanskrit learning. Said to be the permanent abode of Lord Shiva, it has also been the home of influential thinkers like Patanjali, the Buddha, Shankaracharya, Tulsi Das, Kabir Das and many others. Ideas which established

The naga *ascetic, Mahant Keshawa Nand Giri of Gwalior greeting the rising sun in a yogic posture. He is in his 'childlike form' and would object to being called naked.* Naga *ascetics are allowed to cover themselves with an unstitched cloth but on special occasions and while performing rituals, they are 'sky-clad'.*

themselves here inevitably influenced life in the rest of the subcontinent.

Today, the real Varanasi is to be seen as much with the mind's eye as with the physical one. In other words, the city is best understood in intellectual and religious terms rather than historical or political ones.

The Hindus think of the city as a great *tirtha*. The term means a ford or a crossing and is used to describe holy places. It is believed that the city is so charged with holy power that it enables the believer to easily cross over from the material world to the spiritual.

Varanasi has been able to survive the ravages of time because it lives through its hoary myths which underlie every pursuit of its citizen and which strongly influence their psychological, moral and social behaviour. There is a remarkable congruence between mythic structures and social structures; what the myth emphasizes, the cultural system of the city underscores.

The city lives so much in and through mythology that some believe that the real Varanasi is actually invisible to the eye and can only be seen with the eyes of faith.

References to the city are to be found in almost all the ancient Sanskrit texts, but the two main works which are exclusively devoted to the holy city are *Kashi Khanda* of *Skanda Purana* and *Kashi Rahasya* of *Brahmavaivarta Purana*. Lord Shiva inevitably plays a prominent part in most of the myths connected with the city.

According to the myths, the city is located on the trident of Lord Shiva and constitutes the still centre of the world, transcending the perpetual ravages of time, the cycle of creation and dissolution.

It is said that this is the city of joy to which Lord Shiva brought his beautiful bride Parvati, the daughter of the King of the Himalaya, and that now it is the permanent home of the divine couple.

This is the place from where creation began and that this is the place which will survive after doomsday.

It is said that this is the place where the four *purusharthas* (aims of life) of *kama* (sensual pleasure), *artha* (wealth and power), *dharma* (religious duties) and *moksha* (liberation from the cycle of birth and death) are brought to fruition as nowhere else.

Pages 20-21: *A tranquil timelessness pervades as a group of women, immersed in the holy waters of the Ganga, pray together.* ***Facing page:*** *One of the names of Shiva is Pashupati, 'Lord of the Animals'. Here a goat seems to have decided to pay homage to the great god.*

An image of Goddess Kali, the fierce and bloody consort of Shiva. She represents the female energy of the Lord, and is often the centre of esoteric tantric sects.

The Ganga is sacred everywhere in India, for the Hindus believe that it is the river of heaven brought to the earth by King Bhagirathi. However, it is especially sacred at Varanasi, the permanent abode of Lord Shiva. The spiritual power of a ritual bath in the Ganga at Varanasi is said to wash away the sins of many a life time.

The city is said to contain everything that is holy and auspicious. All the 330 million gods of the Hindu pantheon and all the *tirthas* or the holy places of the subcontinent are said to be present in the city. The spiritual power of all the other holy places has been assimilated here and is refracted to the pilgrim who visits it. A visit to the holy *tirtha* of Kashi is equivalent to visiting all the other *tirthas* of the subcontinent.

Facing page: *In an average Hindu household, though tradition gives more importance to men, it is the women who are generally more informed about day to day religious matters and who ensure that rituals are performed regularly and religious practices followed scrupulously. It is their piety that keeps the spirit of Hinduism alive. A group of women returning from their early morning dip in the Ganga engage in ritual prayer.*

An oft witnessed gesture on the river-front: the sacred water is collected in the cup of the hand and then poured back into the river, a ritual offering to the gods.

It is said that this is the city of light which destroys the darkness of ignorance and reveals the truth. Here Lord Shiva bestows on the dying the wisdom which leads to liberation from the endless cycle of birth and death. In short, it is the best place to live in and the best place to die.

Over the years, the people of Varanasi have evolved a distinctive style of living with emphasis on ideas like *fakkadpana*, *masti* and *mauj*. All these terms signify a state

A ghatia*—a Brahmin priest sitting under his picturesque wooden umbrella, is an inseparable part of the river-front. Here he is seen ministering to pilgrims. He performs bathing rituals, applies* tilak *(the sandalwood mark) on the forehead and accepts* daan, *the ritual gift for services rendered.*

gurjari
10%
30%
जबरदस्त • बम्पर • छूट

40
FOUR DECADES OF CLASS
GWALIOR SUITING
सम्राट
मंगलम
98.2%
Satisfied customers
UPTRON
मेरा अपना

of being opposed to cynicism, depression and neurosis and imply a commitment to a carefree, casual and joyous acceptance of life. A true citizen of Banaras will carry the stamp of his city wherever he goes. He lives in the present, untroubled by the past, unworried about the future, enjoying life to the fullest. His is a large and spreading ease born of the conviction that Shiva is in heaven, and heaven is none other than his own beloved city.

In modern times, however, old Varanasi—its beliefs, its customs, its way

Pages 30-31: *The most crowded spot in an overcrowded city—an overview of the Godowlia Crossing, Varanasi's main market.*

Facing page: *Music is an integral part of life in the city. For centuries now the city has been alive with the sound of* bhajan *and* kirtan *(devotional songs),* mushaira *(musical performances by courtesans) and the daily* riyaz *(practice sessions) of some of the greatest names in the annals of Indian music. The living greats from Varanasi include Pandit Ravi Shankar, the sitar maestro and Ustad Bismillah Khan, who plays the shehnai. Here, a shehnai player practices in the early morning light.*

A devotee applying sandlewood paste on his arm after the holy dip in the Ganga.

of life—is under attack and it is possible for a visitor to witness here, as perhaps nowhere else in the country, the intensely dramatic encounter between India's age old traditions and the forces of modernity.

The impact of parliamentary democracy, television and video, the development of tourism and telecommunications, the craze for the English language, all ensure that the conflict between the old and the new, between ancient tradition and modern mores is enacted everyday in Varanasi in different spheres of life.

In the labyrinth of the narrow lanes of Varanasi, time itself seems to have lost its way. Past, present and future are indistinguishable

Facing page: *The very narrowness of the labyrinthine lanes—called* galis*— has kept modernity at bay and gone a long way in preserving the distinctive identity of the city. A view of a typical Banarasi* gali.

Right: *Detail from a traditional folk painting, decorating a doorway.*

Facing page: *A late evening view of the ghats on the occasion of Kartik Purnima—a full moon festival celebrated in October/ November. The entire river front is illuminated with little clay oil lamps.*

Devotees paying homage to the image of Durga on the occasion of Durga Puja. Like Kali, Durga too is a fierce manifes tion of the female energy of Lord Shiva, and is specially popular among Bengalis.

Facing page: *Lolarka Kund ('The Well of the Trembling Sun') is probably the most ancient of the sacred sites of Varanasi. Dedicated to sun worship, it is visited mainly by couples seeking the boon of a male child.*

If Lord Shiva is the king, then goddess Annapurna is the queen of Varanasi and she provides food and abundance to the citizens. Annapurna means 'plenteous food' and on the day of Annakuta, the festival dedicated to her, food and sweets of all kinds are distributed. An entire temple made up of sweets has been erected for the occassion in the Annapurna Temple.

❖ RAM

The Ram Lila, based on the Hindu epic the *Ramayana*, is an integral part of the festival of Dussehra (September-October) which celebrates the victory of Lord Ram over the demon Ravan.

The Ram Lila performed at Ram Nagar, the township located on the other bank of the Ganga, is famous throughout the country and attracts vast crowds. It lasts for thirty-one days.

During the performance of the Ram Lila different parts of Ram Nagar are imaginatively

transformed into the various places associated with the story of Ram. Thus, one locality becomesAyodhaya, the birth place of Ram, and another becomes the forest where Ram was exiled. The actors, the musicians and the audience move from one place to another performing scenes from the *Ramayana* in the appropriate setting.

Traditionally, the kings of Varanasi have been closely associated with the Ram Lila of Ram Nagar. Even today, the Maharaja of Banaras attends the performances in full state.

and the mythical, the historical and the contemporary exists simultaneously. Somewhere at the centre of it all are answers to fundamental questions like: What is India? Where is it headed? How is the past being adapted to meet the needs of the future and what is it that is being lost and what is being gained?

Pages 40-41: *A joyous throng of women having their ritual bath on the occasion of the festival of Daalchanth. The primary religious requirement is for bathers to greet the rising sun half-immersed in water. Often the pilgrims spend the entire night at the ghats, to immerse themselves at first light.*

Facing page: *Not for the faint hearted—this typical Varanasi dive from the top of a temple at Scindia Ghat.*

Brahmin priests grinding sandalwood paste to anoint the foreheads of devotees. Every pilgrim likes to have the tilak *(mark of the sandalwood paste) put on his forehead. It signifies purity.*

अहिल्याबाई घाट

SILK FACTORY

Pages 46-47: *The force of faith that has for two and a half millennia drawn pilgrims from all over India to Varanasi is astonishing—and inspiring. The river front provides an unending spectacle of human activity.*

Facing page: *The gold plated Kashi Vishvanath Temple, popularly known as the Golden Temple, is the centre of Shiva worship not just in the city, but in north India. Thousands pay homage to the Shiva linga here every day. In the background is the Gyan Vapi mosque built by the Emperor Aurangzeb on the ruins of the old Vishvanath Temple. The present temple is a comparatively recent construction, built by Rani Ahilya Bai Holkar of Indore in the eighteenth century.*

The Shiva linga at Madhyameshwara temple—the 'Lord of the Centre'—one of the ancient sacred sites, mentioned in the Puranas.

Facing page: *A unique idol, embodying the different facets of the Lord.*

Ganesha, 'Remover of Obstacles', is given the pride of place in any act of ritual worship. Considered to be the son of Lord Shiva, the elephant-headed god is one of the favourite deities of the citizens of Varanasi, and one encounters his shrine on almost every street corner.

The impressive Ram Nagar Fort, built in the seventeenth century, is located across the river. For generations now, it has housed the kings of Varanasi. It has a small museum displaying the household goods of former kings.

The erstwhile Maharaja of Varanasi—Shri Vibhuti Narain Singh.

An athlete performing a difficult exercise in an akhara. *The* akhara *or gymnasium is a venerable Banarasi institution where weight-lifting, mud wrestling and elaborate massages are practiced by young and old.*

The paan *symbolizes the Banarasi's addiction to the good things of life. A Banarasi takes infinite pains over its preparation and a true Banarasi can be identified from the way in which he makes, receives and offers* paan.

A view of the Manikarnika, also known as the Burning Ghat, India's most famous cremation ground. It is believed that anyone cremated here achieves moksha. *Hindus bring their near and dear ones from all over the country for the last rites. The holy flame to light the pyres has been kept alive here for hundreds of years.*

At Varanasi, the river-front challenges one to comprehend the bewildering variety of India at a single glance. It attracted in the past and continues to attract today, devotees from all parts of the country. The very gods, they say, come to bathe in the Ganga at Varanasi.

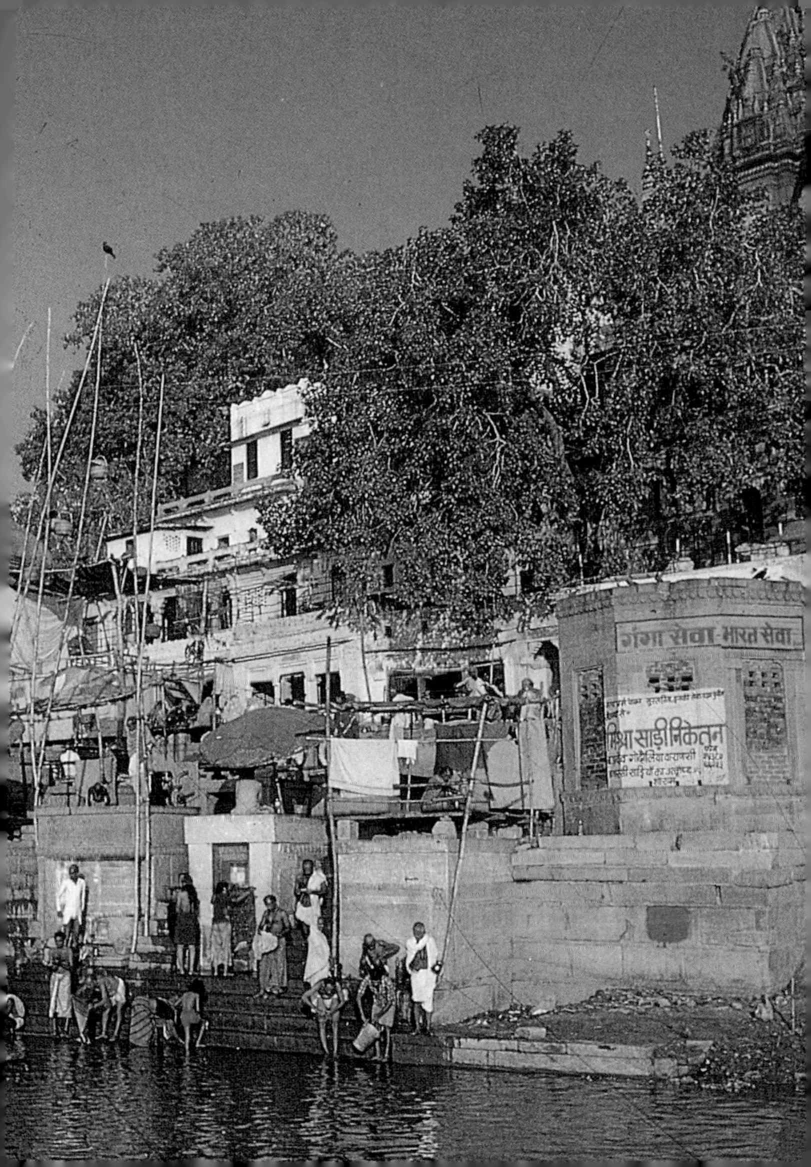
गंगा सेवा - भारत सेवा
श्रा साड़ी निकेतन

2500 years ago the Buddha preached his first sermon at Sarnath, a tiny hamlet 10 kilometres north of Varanasi. This impressively serene statue of the Buddha is housed in the temple called Mool Gandh Koot Vihar.

he Dhameka tupa at Sar-ath, was ected by mperor shoka 272-32 BC). he site of e stupa is elieved be the lace here Buddha preached his second sermon to his first five disciples.

Overleaf: *The unique Bharat Mata (Mother of India) Temple enshrines a detailed map of India, carved in marble, in the inner sanctum.*